Pure
Manhood

JASON EVERT

Catholic Answers
San Diego
2007

Pure Manhood
Jason Evert
© 2007 Catholic Answers, Inc.

Published by Catholic Answers, Inc.
2020 Gillespie Way
El Cajon, California 92020
888-291-8000 (orders)
619-387-0042 (fax)
www.catholic.com

NIHIL OBSTAT: I have concluded that the materials presented in this work are free of doctrinal and moral errors.
Bernadeane M. Carr, SLT
March 6, 2007

IMPRIMATUR: In accord with 1983 CIC 827 § 3, permission to publish this work is hereby granted.
Robert H. Brom
Bishop of San Diego
March 6, 2007

Cover by Devin Schadt
Printed in the United States of America
ISBN 978-1-933919-05-8

I was unloading a surfboard from the roof of my truck when I heard a mumbled voice behind me say, "Man, chicks are sooo easy!" I looked down and saw a guy about my age, hung over and half asleep in the back seat of his convertible. Apparently, he had been unable to drive home after his date the previous evening. Unsure of what to say to him, I took my board and walked to the beach.

Sitting on the water that afternoon, I did more thinking than surfing. I thought of the times I had used girls and the times that I had felt used by them. I thought of the times that I was congratulated for my impurities and mocked for the innocence I managed to retain. A quote I once read echoed in my head: "Until a man knows he's a man, he will be trying to prove that he is one."[1]

What does it mean to be a man? How does a guy establish his manhood?

Most of us learned in the locker room that losing your purity proves your masculinity. But we all know that something is missing from this picture of manhood. Behind all the bragging about sexual conquests on prom night, every guy harbors a deeper longing to cherish a girl. For example, when a guy imagines his future bride, he doesn't think about "getting some" from her. He thinks about giving his life to her.

Despite what the world seems to think, most guys are not players who intentionally victimize clueless women. Sure, those guys exist. But nowadays it seems like there are just as many girls out there who are using guys. There is a battlefield of love and lust within everyone's heart. Thankfully, our call to love runs deeper than our temptation to lust. For proof of this, one need only look as far as the outside of a strip club. There will be a neon sign claiming that there are "gentlemen" inside. No matter how far we fall, we never forget that we are supposed to be men.

The purpose of this booklet is to help you to choose the good and live it out. It is not a condemnation but a challenge to accept the demands of authentic manhood and, in doing so, to become a blessing to women and a visible image of God the Father's love.

"What do girls want?"

To answer this question, I gave a survey to a thousand high school and college girls. Two of the four questions I asked were "What do you want in a man?" and "If you wanted guys to know one thing, what would it be?"

Here's what they said:

The quality they most wanted in a man was that he be faithful and honest. In a close second, they wanted him to be respectful. Other common responses were that the man be loving, caring, pure, and close to God. Together, these six virtues accounted for about 90 percent of the votes. Attractiveness, athletic ability, and wealth were not the first concerns.

When asked about the one thing they wanted men to know, some of the ladies offered pearls of wisdom such as "Don't be stupid" and "Never say, 'She looks fat in that dress.'" Fortunately, most of the girls gave more substantial answers about what they like guys to know.

Some suggested, "Take a chance," when it comes to relationships, or "Be the person you want to marry." A large number of young women said, "Be yourself, and don't let your friends pressure you into becoming anyone else." Some said, "Love God more than me."

Other girls expressed their hurts and insecurities. They wanted guys to know "We're fragile," "Never hurt me," or "If I could take back one night, I would." These answers conveyed a sense that many girls had been manipulated and used and few had been guarded in love or pursued with sincerity. Many seemed to doubt that they're worth fighting for.

Purity was a common theme in 20 percent of the responses, with girls saying things like "Never pressure a girl," "It's more hot to wait until you're married," and "I am waiting for you, and when I find you some day I'll give you all of myself because I've saved myself for you. I love you wherever you are and whoever you are!" One girl addressed purity of speech, saying, "Don't say perverted things to girls. It's degrading and scary." Another girl said, "If you're trying to be pure and you see a girl dressed modestly, tell her you appreciate her modesty."

But the top response by a landslide—representing 429 of 1,000 answers—was that the girls wanted a man to know how to treat her like a lady. They expressed the hope that guys would respect women and not use them, and "Love me for who I am, not just my body." The girls also asked not to be treated like "one of the guys." In the words of one girl, "All that girls want is a gentleman." By *gentleman* she did not mean a sweet and thoughtful boy but rather a man who knows how to honor a woman properly.

Knowing this, it's reasonable to ask why girls date jerks if they really want gentlemen. Or why they dress like they want their bodies to get all the attention if they really want guys to be interested in their personalities.

One young woman answered these objections best when she wrote, "Some of us don't know how we should be treated." Sometimes girls are willing to forget their dignity and their deepest longings for the sake of feeling desirable to a man. In a similar way, we may forget our desire to be gentlemen for the sake of receiving pleasure.

"What's a gentleman supposed to do?"

Guys are constantly told to act like gentleman but are rarely told exactly what this means. I include the following not because I've mastered any of it, but because I could have used these specifics a while ago.

If you're interested in a girl, first build the foundation of a lasting friendship. By doing this, you'll be able to see if you're attracted to her personality and not just her looks. It will also give you the chance to know her family before you pursue her. When a guy skips this step of a relationship, the girl's parents often resent him and wonder why he's afraid to be around them. They know that a guy who isn't trustworthy is easily intimidated by loving parents. They want only the best for their daughter, and if you love her, you will share their intention. I once heard a mother say that she was so protective of her daughter because after working so hard to raise godly children, the last thing she wanted was to see her daughter throw it all away and marry some "unprepared spiritual midget."

When the time comes to ask a young woman out, take the initiative. There's no way around it—a guy has to experience being a nervous wreck as he asks a girl out. This honors the girl, because it takes the burden of rejection off of her and places it on you. By initiating love, you're telling her that you'd rather be rejected by her than not have had the chance to win her. So get out of your shell. If she's not worth the pain of rejection, then you don't desire her enough.

Plan ahead for your date. Show that you've put some thought and effort into making the time with her special. Don't just sit there saying, "I don't know. What do *you* want to do?" If you go to a restaurant, open the door for her. When you sit down, pull her chair out for her. Deliberately give her the seat that faces the center of the restaurant, or whichever one has the better view. You should take the seat that faces the wall. This is a sign that you won't be looking over her shoulder at the hostess or the TV during dinner. Your eyes are on her, and she knows it. If an attractive woman walks by, you should keep your attention on your date, so that she is secure in your love. Staring at other women while you're on a date shows a lack of respect, self-control, and class.

When the waiter comes, let her order first. When the food arrives, pray grace, and don't eat as if someone is about to take your dinner away from you. Take your time, and don't swipe food off of her plate unless she offers. When it comes to talking, avoid conversations that sound like, "I've talked enough about me. Now *you* talk about me." Take an interest in her. Keep the conversation pure, avoid gossip, and be considerate about what she may not want to discuss. When the bill comes, look at it with wide eyes and slide it over to her, and say, "If I were you, I wouldn't pay that much." Not really. If you've invited her out to a meal, you should pay.

If you're getting the feeling that you're becoming a servant, you're getting the right idea. If you hope to be a father one day (as a dad or a priest), then get used to it. The man is the spiritual head of the family. Paul tells husbands that they should be the head of their wives as Christ was the head of the Church, and that they should love their brides as Christ loved the Church (Eph. 5). But don't confuse leadership with domination. Remember that Christ was the one who washed his disciples' feet and that he was crucified for them. In the same way, the man is to be the leader by serving. Although you are not the spiritual leader of your date, you can still take the initiative to honor her in many ways.

It has been said that beginning at the age of two, women speak three times as many words as guys do. I don't doubt this for a second. But one problem this causes in relationships is that we don't talk. As the relationship deepens, let her know—in words—where you stand. Sometimes a girl will lie awake at night pulling her hair out trying to figure out if a guy likes her, while he's lying in bed wondering how to get to the next level of his video game. Be clear with her. I don't mean that you have to pour out your dreams of the future, which feature her driving a minivan filled with your offspring. Just let her know where you're at. I can think of several times when I was initially interested in a girl, spent some time with her, got disinterested, and moved on—all without ever having the courtesy to talk to her about it until I dropped the "let's just be friends" bomb.

"How far is too far?"

Imagine yourself at home alone with a beautiful girlfriend, sitting on the couch. She leans towards you, gazes into your eyes, and your heart begins to race. You love each other deeply and have been together for a long time. How far should you go? Where do you draw the line?

Before you answer the question, let's change one detail of the scenario. Instead of you and your girlfriend, let's say the guy is someone you hardly know and the girl is your little sister. Now, where did you say you wanted to draw the line?

You guard your sister's innocence because you love her. Why don't we do the same for the girlfriends we claim to love so deeply? We have all kinds of reasons to justify our actions. We tell ourselves, "She's okay with it," "It's not like we're going all the way," or "I can see myself marrying her one day." If you've convinced yourself that a form of physical affection is okay, try picturing the expression on her dad's face if he walked into the room while you were doing it.

The bottom line is this: Until her father gives you her hand in marriage, he is her man. Although my wife's dad abandoned her when she was little, her foster-father walked her down the aisle on our wedding day, gave me a firm handshake, and entrusted her to me. Honor a girl's dad in the same way you will want to be honored when it's your daughter going to the prom with a teenage guy you barely know. Ask yourself: Would I want a guy like me dating my own daughter? Or my sister?

If you are being called to marriage, imagine that your future wife is on a date right now with a guy you'll never meet. How far would you like the two of them to go? Odds are that you'd like her to be just as pure after the date as she was before it.

Most guys—if they're honest with themselves—will admit that they have one standard for their sisters, future wives, and future daughters but an entirely different standard for themselves. To avoid this double standard, treat girls the way you would want a guy to treat your future bride. Then, even if a relationship doesn't work out, your girlfriend will be a better person for having dated you. She won't feel regretful or resentful. She'll be closer to God and to her family, not alienated from them.

These guidelines may clarify some things, but they don't get to the heart of the matter. If we love girls, why would we ask how close to sin we can get them? We should be more interested in how close to God we can lead them. Purity is not about following a list of rules so that we'll avoid hell. It's about wanting heaven for the women we love.

"What if I really love her?"

Let's define *love* to answer that question. Pope John Paul II explained it best when he wrote, "Love is not merely a feeling; it is an act of will that consists of preferring, in a constant manner, the good of others to the good of oneself."[2]

How does that apply to our relationships? Think about this.

Research collected from over 10,000 women revealed that the sooner a girl becomes sexually active, the more likely she is to suffer the following:

- Out-of-wedlock pregnancy
- Single motherhood
- STDs
- Multiple sexual partners
- Breakups
- Abortion
- Poverty
- Depression
- Divorce

This research shows that the longer a woman delays sexual activity, the greater the quality of life she enjoys.[3] If a young man really loves a girl, he would never risk harming her.

Consider the words of St. John Chrysostom as an example of such love. He said that a young husband should say to his bride, "I have taken you in my arms, and I love you, and I prefer you to my life itself. For the present life is nothing, and my most ardent dream is to spend it with you in such a way that we may be assured of not being separated in the life reserved for us."[4] This is love: when no pleasure on earth could be more desirable than wanting to be with a woman for eternity.

The quality of a man's love for a woman can be measured by his feeling of responsibility for her. We've all been told as young men that if we want to become a "man," one way to do it is at the expense of a woman. But God tells us that manhood will come only at our own expense—in this case, for the sake of a woman. If I don't suffer for her sake, she will suffer for mine. If a man says he loves a woman, but has no desire to protect her body or soul, then his "love" is only for pleasure.

We know deep down that the only way a man is able receive a woman fully is if he has given himself to her fully. Then, as her husband, he has the privilege of becoming one with her. Wait for her. If God wills it, he will give her to you. The wait may be difficult, but if you truly love her, then you know that love is capable of very heroic acts. And if you don't think she's worth waiting for, why are you with her?

"If she's willing to do it, why is it wrong?"

Most guys assume that as long as a girl consents, they've done nothing wrong. Without realizing it, many of us share this mentality: "As long as I don't force her, it's okay."

Yet often after going too far with a girl, we go away feeling empty. We know we've misused our God-given power to lead. One college football player told me that he would initiate sexual things with his girlfriend, "But sometimes afterwards, I feel as though I almost raped her. I mean I know I didn't, but it's not like she wanted to before we started. I just keep on pushing the envelope until she wants to."

But plenty of girls do not simply go along with it—they take the initiative and pressure the guy. Opportunities like this are the most difficult to resist, because immediate gratification awaits you, and all you need to do is go along. It is at times like this when a man's strength or weakness becomes evident. When a woman is willing to be impure, the man who loves her must have enough control over his body and enough concern for her soul to tell her no. It is one of the clearest marks of authentic manhood: being able to see a woman's dignity, especially when she does not. He knows he has no right to see her body, even though she has surrendered it. A true man will not take advantage of a woman who does not know her worth.

Unfortunately, young men rarely hear about other guys practicing such self-restraint. No one ever bragged in the locker room about saying no to his girlfriend or his date. In fact, how many guys do you know who have *ever* said no to a girl? One would think that we're expected to take everything she's willing to give us.

It seems that most girls need a reason to have sex, while most guys need a reason *not* to have sex. Unless we're deeply convinced of the value of purity, we see no reason to preserve it. But through the battle for purity, a guy comes to appreciate a woman as a gift to be received, not a goal to be conquered.

We know inside that it's more masculine to guard a girl's innocence than to damage it. After all, which demands more strength? Obviously it's easier to wear down a girl with your words than it is to preserve your purity. The easy choice only requires her to be weak. The harder choice demands that you be strong.

"Is she going to think something's wrong with me if I say no?"

That depends on what kind of girl she is. One young woman told me that she cried when her boyfriend said he wanted to stop having sex, because she thought he was breaking up with her. But then, she said, "He reassured me that this wasn't the case and that he still loved me and wanted to love me for my mind and not just my body. I was overwhelmed by this."

It's surprisingly rare for a woman to look down on a guy who wants to guard the innocence of the relationship. To test this, I asked the thousand young women in my survey the following question: "If you were going too far with a guy, and he gave you a kiss on the forehead and said, 'I think we need to slow down. I respect you too much to do all this with you, and I want to fall in love with you for all the right reasons,' would you find him more attractive, or less attractive?"

Almost 100 percent of the girls—995—said that they would find the guy *more* attractive. One girl said this was "because he was thinking about us and not just him." Another girl remarked, "I'm not going to lie. At first, I would be thinking, 'What? What kind of guy says that?' But then later that night I would be thinking, 'I really like this guy.'"

I posed a final question to these girls: "Some guys fear that being a virgin is embarrassing. How would you feel if a guy saved his virginity for you, his bride?" Again, the responses overwhelmingly indicated the attractiveness of purity. Here are some of their replies:

- "He is the kind of guy I'd need to snatch up before the rest of the billions of girls did."
- "Stop worrying about what others say. It means so much if you wait!"
- "That is hot."
- "It's okay to be a virgin. In fact, most girls prefer it."
- "It takes a lot for a guy to stay a virgin, and I love boys like that—who don't care what people think!!!"
- "He's more manly than most guys."
- "They shouldn't be embarrassed. I'm not."
- "His bride is going to be lucky."
- "Thank God for guys like him."
- "A lot of girls like myself find it geeky when a guy is scared if he's a virgin. He should be proud."
- "I'd feel like a true princess, because that's how I want to feel on my wedding night."
- "I'd want him more!"
- "This is the most beautiful thing a man can give his bride. It sums up the essence of being a man in one choice. He has promised his whole self, including his body."
- "Awesome. I won't feel like I'm with all his past girlfriends."
- "He can respect you more if he respects himself."

Almost every girl—996—said that she would feel loved, honored, and more attracted to such a man. Of the remaining four, one expressed disbelief, and three others were indifferent, saying things like "I would love him no more or less if he did."

Every girl longs to know that she's lovable, desirable, and worth protecting. By the time a girl gets to college, she has often given up hope because of the things she's seen (or done). She may settle for hookups or being "friends with benefits," but in her heart, she dreams of something more. In fact, more college women than I can count ask me the very same question: "All the guys are interested in only one thing. Where can I find a decent man?"

Imagine if you were to tell such a girl that you didn't want to do something sexual. If she leaves you because you want to be pure, then you know she never loved you to begin with, and you're better off without her. But if she stays with you, then you'll respect each other all the more. Either way, we must all face our fear of rejection if we're ever going to love.

As the survey showed, most women long to find a confident man who is capable of self-restraint. Even if you've already lost your virginity, you can still choose to start over and live the virtue of purity. Regardless of the past, it's never too late to become the man you ought to be.

"What's wrong with thinking about it?"

God wants us to think about sex. Yes, you read that correctly. Unfortunately, guys almost never think about sex. They joke about it and dream about it, but they rarely actually stop and *think* about it. What is it? Who invented it?

To see God's original design for the gift of sex, we need to go back to the beginning, when sexual desire was experienced in a totally pure way. When Adam first saw Eve, his urge toward her was not felt as a selfish desire to take. Rather, he saw his call to love her. In fact, it was her naked body that revealed his call to make a total gift of himself to her. By doing so, together they imaged the very love of God. God's love is free, total, faithful, and life-giving, and so was theirs.

But the question really is: "What's wrong with fantasizing about sex, as long as I'm not actually doing it?" Actually, the fact that you're not doing it is part of the problem. If you're doing something sexual, you should be doing it as God intended. But we often turn away from our call to love and settle for its counterfeit, which is lust.

In the midst of your temptations, you must not forget that sexual desire is a gift from God. Being sexually attracted to beautiful women is not a sign that something is wrong with you. In fact, it's proof that something is right with you. Unfortunately, many guys assume that purity is unattainable because they do not understand the difference between sexual desire and lust. Since they can't prevent themselves from being sexually attracted and experiencing temptation, they think they're failing at chastity. So they despair, give up, and assume that God has a cruel sense of humor, giving men hormones and then expecting them not to think about sex.

But purity of heart does not eliminate sexual attraction. The pure man experiences the same desires as any other guy, but he refuses to let the beauty of a woman's body distract him from the dignity she deserves. A lustful man, on the other hand, takes the beauty of a woman's body and places it above the value of the woman herself.

When temptation occurs, a decision must be made. When you begin to entertain thoughts of using a girl and seeing her as an object, you have given in. Think of it this way: Sexual attraction is the invitation. Lust is when we accept it wrongfully, outside of our call to love.

If you begin to accept such invitations, you will find, as St. Augustine did, that "lust indulged became habit, and habit unresisted became necessity."[5] He knew that our minds are not content with merely thinking about sex, just as our eyes are not satisfied with looking. God has designed our sexual desires to be all-consuming; if we arouse our desires, we will want to fulfill them.

The more we indulge in sexual thoughts and actions, the more difficult it is to stop them. It's easy to stop a train when the wheels begin to roll, but it takes a long time to stop it when it hits full speed. In the same way, the most crucial battle for our purity occurs when the temptation first appears. The more we give in, the weaker our wills become.

If you can control your thoughts about women, you'll control your words, your eyes, and your actions. God cares about the purity of your thoughts because they reveal the state of your heart. Whatever wins the heart—purity or lust—will win the thoughts, the words, the body, and the soul for eternity.

"How are you supposed to keep your mind pure?"

Temptation will always be there, especially in view of the way most girls dress today. But the strongest sexual temptations usually come during the teenage years, and they may be made even stronger by the environment in which a guy places himself. When I was in high school, I thought it was difficult to be pure—but I had immersed myself in porn, had friends who always talked about sexual stuff, listened to music that glorified meaningless sex, and spent countless hours watching television. Compared to the small amount of time I spent in prayer, it shouldn't have been a surprise to me that my soul felt weak compared to the strength of my lust.

Sometimes we think, "Okay, God. I'll be pure as soon as you take away my sexual desires." But it doesn't work that way. If we look for solid friends, trash the porn, guard our eyes while watching television, get rid of music that degrades women, and deepen our prayer lives, temptations will occur less frequently and will be easier to overcome. The truth is that we have more control over the situation than we like to admit.

Let's say you try all this. Impure thoughts will still come, but God will not judge you for what suddenly pops into your mind. Imagine that you're watching a basketball game on television, and the camera zooms in on a cheerleader who can't seem to afford any food or clothing. Your mind will respond to that image more quickly than to speech or reason, because when you see a sexual image your involuntary nervous system responds instantly. In about a third of a second, excitatory neurotransmitters flood your brain, sending hormones surging through the bloodstream, dilating your pupils, flushing your skin, increasing your heart rate, and changing your muscle tone. You sense her vulnerability subconsciously.

Before you've had a chance to think about the morality of what you're seeing, your body has already reacted. That is sexual desire, and we should not think of it as sinful. That first temptation was beyond your control. All God looks at is how you respond. Some people suggest you try to think about something other than the woman tempting you. You can certainly remove the image that's tempting you, but what do you do with the thought that's still in your head? Instead of trying to bury your temptation, lift it up. Think about the woman, but instead of lusting after her, pray for her. Ask God to help you see her as he sees her.

The point of purity is not to repress our desires and act like they don't exist, but to acknowledge their power and beg for the strength to love as God loves. If we do this, our sexuality won't be something we hide from God. Instead, he will shine through us onto the women we love.

"What's wrong with porn? You're not hurting anyone."

When an Alaskan Eskimo becomes aware of the presence of a wolf in his territory, he is forced to protect his herds and children. But rather than face the wolf directly, the hunter uses the animal's own appetite to bring it down. He begins by slaughtering one of his smaller goats and pouring its blood over the blade of a knife. The weapon is left to freeze in the arctic temperatures. Once the first coat is set, more blood is poured on the knife and frozen. This process is repeated until the entire blade is thickly coated with frozen blood.

Before nightfall, the Eskimo hikes outside his camp and buries the handle of the knife in the ground, with the blade protruding from the snow. Since wolves can smell blood from miles away, it doesn't take long for one to track the scent and cautiously begin to lick the frozen blood. As the taste excites the animal, it begins to lick more aggressively.

Before long, part of the blade is exposed and the wolf's tongue is nicked. But since its tongue has been numbed by the icy blood, the animal is unaware of the damage that's been caused. As more goat's blood is cleaned off the blade, it is replaced with the warmer blood of the wolf. In an excited frenzy at the taste of fresh blood, the animal licks more ravenously, is cut again and again, and continues to bleed until it becomes faint. Within hours, the wolf will die of blood loss.

This trap is like the allure of pornography. You experience satisfaction without consequences, and you feel like you're getting away with it—for a while. But before you realize it, the damage has been done. This is always the case with sin: It promises us everything and gives us nothing.

In the case of porn, the most troubling effects usually come later in life, when you actually try to love a woman. Research about people who looked at porn found that they were less likely to be satisfied with their partner's affection, physical appearance, sexual curiosity, and sexual performance.[6] Some husbands even come to think that they have the right to be aroused by fantasies. They seem to feel that if a wife isn't flawless, it's her fault.

As one high school student said to me, "Imagine if the first woman's body you saw was your wife's. Marriage would be as exciting as porn!"

Our minds are like a clean canvas, given to us by God. On it, we're free to place whatever image we want of womanhood. I began shaping my expectations of a woman's body with swimsuit magazines and porn long before high school. By the time I graduated, I assumed that my warped view of women was normal. I began to look at them like I would browse though a catalogue of truck parts: That one has a nice off-road package. This one has better shocks. I like the rims on that one! I judged the value of a woman by how much lust I felt for her. The sight of a beautiful woman automatically triggered a lustful thought.

At the time, I never knew that although the images took only seconds to see, they would take years to forget. As my eyes passed from one image to the next, I had no idea of the impact this would have on my mind. The pleasure center of a man's brain is called the medial preoptic nucleus, and it is easily trained.

When a man experiences sexual pleasure, he trains his brain to associate whatever he is looking at or doing with sexual joy. In the case of porn, the man's mind is trained to associate sexual joy with hundreds of forbidden fantasies.

How is a man supposed to live this way for years, and then suddenly shift gears and jump into a healthy and holy marriage? If a man never learns to say no to his lust, when the day comes for love, his lust may destroy it.

The brain can be retrained, but the process takes years. So begin now. Trash the porn, but don't stop there. In the words of Pope John Paul II, God "assigned as a duty to every man the dignity of every woman."[7] Instead of lusting after the women in porn, begin to love them. One way to do this is to stop supporting the industry that degrades them.

If real manhood means denying ourselves for the good of our beloved, porn emasculates us. It teaches us only to take from women. But by removing it from our lives and fighting for the dignity of every woman, we are emptying ourselves and becoming the men of God that women need us to be, and we are no longer emptying them. As St. Josemaria Escriva said, "There is need for a crusade of manliness and purity to counteract and nullify the savage work of those who think man is a beast. And that crusade is *your* work."[8]

"What if it's just a swimsuit magazine?"

Imagine marrying a beautiful woman and celebrating the birth of your first daughter. She looks just like your bride, and you're in love all over again. Years go by, and you begin to raise a family.

Today, it's her seventeenth birthday and she is having a pool party with her friends. She walks out of the house in her bathing suit, and your son takes the opportunity to grab his camera and take some pictures. Since she's so attractive, he sells the pictures online, and she agrees to the arrangement as long as she gets a cut of the money he earns. Before long, thousands of strangers on the Internet are lusting after your princess. They stare at her body, and make sick jokes about what they think of her.

How would you feel?

Now imagine the heart of God the heavenly Father, who loves his daughters infinitely more than you or I could ever love ours. The women in our swimsuit magazines are the daughters of the King of heaven. It's sad that we sons have made a market selling his daughters, our sisters. For this reason, Pope John Paul II challenged us: "Each man must look within himself to see whether she who was entrusted to him as a sister in humanity . . . has not become in his heart an object of adultery."[9]

If a desire to love God and respect women does not motivate you to get rid of swimsuit magazines, consider what will happen if you do not. Do you honestly think that looking at hundreds of perfect female bodies will not affect the way you look at women and shape the expectations you have for your future bride?

I guarantee you that it already has. No matter how attractive a swimsuit model is, you flip the page. She could be the most beautiful woman on earth, but you won't look at her for more than thirty seconds. You're aroused but bored and dissatisfied. You bond and you break. Your standard of physical beauty becomes one of impossible perfection. But if the most seductive supermodels fail to keep your interest for more than a few seconds, how long will your bride hold your attention? You have trained yourself to be a glutton who is never filled.

When you close the magazine and walk out among the public, you assume that constant lust is natural for a guy. Just as your eye wanders with lust from one page to the next in the magazine, your eyes gaze from one girl to the next. When you see girls in school or even at church, you turn them into objects—without even realizing it. You become shallower and shallower and unable to see a woman as God sees her. This is why St. Alphonsus Liguori tells us, "When a raven finds a dead body, its first act is to pluck out the eyes, and the first injury that [impurity] inflicts on the soul is to take away the light of the things of God."[10] Meanwhile, you lull your conscience to sleep, telling yourself that nobody is getting hurt.

Sirach 9:2 says, "Do not give yourself to a woman so that she gains mastery over your strength." But this is exactly what happens when you look at magazines that fuel your lust. If a husband is hooked on such fantasies, he's only a shadow of the man his wife and kids need him to be. In the case of single men, many of them hide in their smutty magazines; the fantasy of having dozens of perfect women at their disposal is more alluring to them than the possibility of rejection by one woman or the burdens of commitment. They turn inward and never experience the joy of sacrificial love because they fear its demands.

"What about masturbation?"

To understand what's wrong with masturbation, we must understand the objective and meaning of sex. God created sex for the purposes of making babies and of bonding. Masturbation achieves neither and reinforces the myth that men need sexual gratification whenever they desire it. If you think about it, masturbation is kind of like birth control for people who don't have a partner. You want the pleasure, but you don't want its life-giving effects.

As for the meaning of sex, look at God's design for it. When a couple is married, they promise at the altar that their love will be free, total, faithful, and open to life. When they make love, they speak those wedding vows with their bodies. Their love is free: It is not coerced or driven by lust. It is total: Until death do they part; they hold nothing back from each other, including their fertility. It is faithful: It includes the mind, eyes, and heart, as well as the body. It is open to life: It is not deliberately sterilized. Consider all that sex is supposed to be; in this light, masturbation is not even a shadow of love.

Masturbation also harms your ability to love because you are bonding with fantasies. During sexual pleasure, the brain releases epinephrine, which helps to imprint sexual images onto your memory. Because God designed you for one woman, he wants sexual images to be burned into your brain. But he wants to brand into your mind the beauty of your wife and her alone. When we turn from his design, we harm ourselves. This is why the Bible says, "Every other sin which a man commits is outside the body; but the immoral man sins against his own body" (1 Cor. 6:18).

If a man never overcomes the habit of masturbation, what will happen if he gets married? Instead of making love, he'll use his wife as an outlet for what he thinks of as his "sexual needs." Prior to marriage, he may think, "Man, it will be nice to get married one day, so that I can experience all this stuff for real." But if he does get married, he'll soon discover that marital sex is not the fulfillment of porn or masturbation. They are a distortion of love—driven by lust and self-ishness instead of love and selflessness.

If you look at the qualities that women look for in a man—courage, selflessness, strength, honor, confidence—you'll notice that masturbation is pretty much the opposite of all of them. Instead of increasing confidence, masturbation weakens a man's idea of himself. Instead of making him courageous and strong, it saps him of his strength.

God has not given us this strong sexual drive so that we would spend it on ourselves and become slaves to our weaknesses. Rather, as Pope John Paul II said long before he became pope:

> God who is Father, who is Creator, planted a reflection of his creative strength and power within man. . . . We should sing hymns of praise to God the Creator for this reflection of himself in us— and not only in our souls but also in our bodies.[11]

Our world desperately needs a renewal of true fatherhood, and no matter what vocation we are called to, we must mature into this role. The idea of becoming a father may seem distant, but the virtues or vices we practice now will shape who we become. Let us begin by battling our selfish tendencies and learning self-mastery. Although masturbation can become a very tempting habit, it can—and must—be overcome.

"What if you have homosexual attractions?"

The world tells people who have same-sex attractions that they have two options: either hide in the closet in fear or come out, embrace your identity, and sleep with whoever you want. Acknowledging your attractions but living a pure life isn't even proposed as a realistic choice, because the world assumes that sex equals love, and no one should have to live without love.

A guy who has these attractions may not want them, or even know where they're coming from. Perhaps they stem from an unhealthy relationship with his father, an inability to relate to other guys, or even sexual abuse. Whatever the case may be, purity will help him understand the origin of his feelings.

Every guy needs male approval as part of becoming a man. But in this need for masculine love, some guys may question their identity and try to find it in sex. But that will not satisfy their calling to make a total gift of themselves. The homosexual act is disordered, much like contraceptive sex between heterosexuals. Both acts are directed against God's natural purpose for sex—babies and bonding.

Even if a person does not believe in God, he cannot argue with nature. For example, the life expectancy of homosexual men is half that of heterosexual men.[12] Furthermore, imagine what would happen if all people with same-sex attractions were placed in their own country. It would be empty in a century, because bodies of the same gender are not made to receive each other. Even if a man has same-sex attractions, his body is heterosexual. He was designed to give life.

If you struggle with same-sex attractions, realize that you are not alone. God loves you and has a plan for your life. The Church has a network of those who carry the same cross and choose to glorify God with their bodies (see www.couragerc.net).

"What about safe sex?"

I recently met a wife who was a virgin when she married, but her husband had slept around. At the time of their wedding, neither of them knew that he was infected with herpes, human papillomavirus (HPV), chlamydia, and gonorrhea. As a result, his wife and their babies were infected with herpes. She underwent treatment to prevent cervical cancer caused by HPV, and she lost her ability to have more children because of the damage the other sexually transmitted diseases had caused to her reproductive organs.

Some guys may read that and assume that "safe sex" would have prevented it. But all four of these STDs can be transmitted during "safe sex." Scientifically speaking, safe sex is a joke. For example, HPV is the most commonly transmitted STD and is spread by skin-to-skin sexual contact in the entire genital region, including the surrounding thighs and groin.[13] Even hand-to-genital contact can spread this STD.[14] The Centers for Disease Control reported to Congress that "most studies on genital HPV infection and condom use did not show a protective effect."[15] It's disappointing that condom labels fail to mention that they offer minimal protection from HPV, especially considering that most sexually active women have been infected with HPV.[16]

Any guy who relies on a condom for protection should meet a friend of mine who used a condom every single time and caused seven pregnancies!

I'd recommend something radically different than the message of "protecting" yourself: Don't protect yourself. Forget yourself, and protect your bride. Protect your future children, should God bless you with them. Protect your bride by waiting for her, and protect your kids by guarding the health of their mother. The only 100 percent safe way to accomplish this is through purity.

Besides, if you have to "protect" yourself at the moment when you're supposedly making a gift of yourself, something is wrong. Why is there fear? Are you afraid that if she conceives, the world will no longer revolve around you? Are you afraid that this is how your firstborn child is going to come into the world? If you are not ready to be a father, then you are not ready for sex. This is why a condom is an external sign of internal egoism: You are protecting *yourself*. Manhood is found in total self-giving, not in hiding behind a barrier. Wait until God blesses you with a bride, and then be free and unafraid to give yourself to her totally.

In the meantime, consider this: If you're being called to marriage, do you want your future bride practicing "safe sex" tonight? Odds are that you'd prefer that she save herself for you. Trust me—she hopes you are doing the same for her.

"Why would God give us all these desires if we're not supposed to act on them?"

Your urges can help train you in love and faithfulness. With chastity, you're able to rise above the urge of your hormones, the invitations on the Internet, the ridicule of your peers, the pressure of a date, or the enticement of an affair in marriage. With chastity, none of these things has control over you, and you are free to love. As the *Catechism of the Catholic Church* says:

> The alternative is clear: either man governs his passions and finds peace, or he lets himself be dominated by them and becomes unhappy.[17]

Our sexual urge has the power for both life and destruction, and every boy who wishes to become a man must learn to use his interior strength. If he does not, he may leave a trail of damaged and discarded women in his wake.

If we resist temptation, we also earn merit in heaven. The Bible assures us that God "will repay everyone according to his works: eternal life to those who seek glory, honor, and immortality through perseverance in good works" (Rom. 2:5–7, NAB). Although temptations may seem overwhelming, St. Paul assured us:

> No temptation has overtaken you that is not common to man. God is faithful, and he will not let you to be tempted beyond your strength, but with the temptation will also provide the way of escape, that you may be able to endure it. (1 Cor. 10:13).

Temptation also gives us an opportunity to pray. Imagine how much more you'd pray if you turned to God at each temptation! Temptation also allows us to grow in humility as we realize how weak we are. When a child senses danger, he clings more tightly to his father. In the same way, our temptations should remind us that we need to be united to God in order to live a pure life.

Finally, temptations give us an opportunity to prove our love for God. In fact, the word *temptation* comes from the Latin *tentare*, which means "to test." Temptation is a test of love. By fighting well, we prove our loyalties and give glory to God. After a temptation, you will be either closer to God or further from him. The choice lies with you. If you choose well, your reward will be nothing less that God himself. As St. Francis of Assisi said, "Temptation overcome is, in a way, a ring with which the Lord espouses the soul of his servant to himself."[18]

"Shouldn't I be free to do whatever I want?"

Which of the following two men is free?

The first man lives by himself and isn't in a relationship because he doesn't want to be tied down by commitment. He often stays out all night, enjoying the fact that he doesn't have to answer to anyone when he comes home. On other nights, he spends hours looking at porn online. In fact, he hasn't gone a week without look at porn for years. Occasionally, he hits a strip club with his friends and drinks as much as he wants. He has one child from a previous relationship, but he's glad that the mother has custody of her, since he saw the unplanned kid as a burden.

The second man is married with three kids. He comes home after work to help his wife bathe the kids and get them ready for bed. He has plenty of friends but isn't able to spend as much time with them as he did when he was a bachelor. As for porn and the temptations of other women in his life, he keeps his eyes on his bride.

The world will tell you that the bachelor is free and the husband is enslaved. But take a deeper look. Unless the first guy changes his life, he will lie on his deathbed one day and realize that he wasted his entire life on himself. He was created to make a gift of himself, but he spent his whole life trying to maximize his personal pleasure. His selfishness blinded him from seeing that there's one thing we desire more than freedom, and that is love. We have been created for love. But this love makes demands on us and comes at a heavy price: It costs us ourselves. This is why so many guys pull back. In the words of one man, "I wanted to look like the knight, but I didn't want to bleed like one."[19]

We need to drop the false notion that freedom means doing whatever we want. Pope John Paul II reminded us:

> If freedom is not used, is not taken advantage of by love, it becomes a negative thing and gives human beings a feeling of emptiness and unfulfillment.[20]

The bachelor mentioned above is not free. He is enslaved by his own lust and selfishness. The husband, who seems tied down, is imaging the love of Christ, who said of his life, "No one takes it from me, but I lay it down of my own accord" (John 10:18). The husband knows that giving away your "freedom" for the sake of love saves you from yourself. It liberates you, because it frees you to love. Whether it's for your wife, your kids, or your God, you surrender your freedom as a gift to others.

We are free to turn down the challenges of love, but we will find true freedom only by accepting them. This is the great paradox of Christianity—unless you empty yourself, you will feel empty; unless you surrender your freedom, you will not find it. When it comes to purity, you must look past the initial fear that you will be missing out on something, because beyond the small sacrifice is a great reward. Once you realize that self-control makes you free to love, you will no longer see purity as a loss. Do not be afraid to be a true gentleman, for as St. Josemaria Escriva assured us, "When you decide firmly to lead a clean life, chastity will not be a burden on you: It will be a crown of triumph."[21]

"How do you know if God wants you to be a priest?"

Life makes no sense without love. In the words of Pope John Paul II:

> Man cannot live without love. He remains a
> being that is incomprehensible for himself—his
> life is senseless—if love is not revealed to him,
> if he does not encounter love, if he does not
> experience it and make it his own, if he does not
> participate intimately in it. This is why Christ the
> Redeemer "fully reveals man to himself."[22]

Christ crucified teaches us what it means to be human: that we will find ourselves only in the fullest giving of ourselves.

How does this apply to the priesthood? A priest has died to himself in order to give life to others. He is rightly called a father, because the gift of his sacrifice brings about children in the faith. By giving up his body for his bride (the Church), he brings life into the family of God. A man does not enter the priesthood as an escape but as a conquest. He does not join the seminary because he can't get a date. He goes because of his love for God and his desire to save souls.

All too often, we think of the priesthood in terms of what is given up. We never pause to think about the blessings received, such as the power to forgive sins and to change mere bread into the flesh of God. In the words of Christ:

> Truly I say to you, there is no one who has left
> house or brothers or sisters or mother or father or

> children or lands, for my sake and for the gospel,
> who will not receive a hundredfold now in this
> time . . . and in the age to come. (Mark 10:29–30)

If you feel a tug toward the consecrated life, don't run from it. It won't disappear. Put aside any fears you may have, and pray a Hail Mary each day to help you discern your vocation. When you feel ready, talk to a priest or youth minister about your feelings. Perhaps you can attend a discernment retreat in your diocese. Doing so does not mean that you're signing up for the seminary; it just means you're open to taking a deeper look. Perhaps you will leave the retreat with a deep sense of peace and the knowledge that the priesthood is not for you. Perhaps you will leave with a great hope that God may be calling you. Either way, we should imitate the courage of Mother Teresa, who said, "Of my free will, dear Jesus, I shall follow you wherever you shall go in search of souls, at any cost to myself and out of pure love of you."[23]

"How do you stay pure?"

The following ten points are a game plan for purity. Without them, I do not know how any of us will succeed. But with them, all things are possible.

1. Admit the problem and set the goal.

By nature, men do not like to admit their problems.

When it comes to impurity, we must pray for the humility to see the state of our souls. We all struggle in this area, and we need God's grace to change.

As for the goal, the Bible tells us that there should not be even a hint of immorality among us (Eph. 5:3). This is certainly difficult, but all men like a good challenge.

If you struggle with porn or masturbation, you may have become so entrenched in these habits that giving them up for years seems impossible. Do not give in to discouragement. Instead, set reachable goals for yourself, such as, "I'm not going to do it for two days, for a week, or for some period of time that I know I can reach." You will gain confidence in your ability to be pure if you focus on the next twenty-four hours instead of the next ten years. God asks only that you be pure one day at a time.

2. Remove the temptation.

If we are serious about living a pure life, we need to take an honest look at when and where we fall. For many guys, it's at home when they're alone and bored after school or work or when they're at their girlfriend's house.

🪶 Regardless of the time or place, if you wish to make purity easier, avoid the situations that are an occasion of sin. Avoid relationships with girls who will only bring out the worst in you. Instead, date a woman with high standards, someone you can see yourself marrying. Talking about standards of purity can be awkward if you hardly know the girl. That's why it's so important to have a solid friendship with a girl before you commit to her.

We all need solid friends. As Proverbs 27:17 says, "Iron sharpens iron, and one man sharpens another." Seek out friendships that will make you stronger, not weaker. I recently met a young man who said it was difficult to stay pure. His friends would get him drunk and then try to get him to lose his virginity to a girl he hardly knew. With friends like this, who needs enemies?

Lastly, get rid of any impure things you own. Without one last look, trash them. If you struggle with Internet porn, get a filter for your computer (www.filterreview. com) or take advantage of an accountability site like Covenanteyes.com. If you take these steps, your temptations will gradually weaken. Imagine your desires if you haven't seen porn in a year. The memories will begin to fade, and the soul will regain its strength.

3. Go to confession.

One way to replace your bad habits with good ones is to go to the sacrament of reconciliation at least once a month. By receiving the sacrament, you not only get your sins removed, you get abundant graces to avoid those sins in the future. Find a good priest who can be your spiritual director, and be open and honest with him. In the words of Pope John Paul II, "In order to see Jesus, we first need to let him look at us."[24]

4. Receive the Eucharist.

Never abandon the Mass. It is the fountain of purity. When Elijah was about to embark on a long journey, an angel said to him, "Arise and eat, else the journey will be too great for you" (1 Kgs. 19:7). In the same way, we need the grace that comes from the Eucharist to persevere in purity.

St. John Chrysostom said, "The Eucharist is a fire that inflames us, that, like lions breathing fire, we may retire from the altar being made terrible to the devil."[25] In the Eucharist, we find every grace that is needed for us to live as angels. If you are able, go to daily Mass. This practice is for those who have nothing better to do—which, in my eyes, is all of us.

It is also good to spend time in adoration before the Blessed Sacrament. Pope John Paul II called it "the school of the Eucharist" where Jesus truly reveals the meaning of manhood.

Understandably, many young men find it hard to relate to Jesus. Christian art so often portrays him with such femininity that he looks as if he'd smell like rose petals if you ever met him. When we hear, "Be like Jesus," it does not appeal to us. It's about as inspiring as being told, "Be a nice boy." But look at a realistic crucifix with Christ's wide-open wounds, with his naked body scourged beyond recognition. This is the price he paid so "that he might present the church to himself in splendor, without spot or wrinkle or any such thing, that she might be holy and without blemish" (Eph. 5:27). He suffered so that his bride, the Church, would be pure, and he calls us to do the same. His example of "This is my body, given up for you" is the antidote to our tendency to look at girls and think, "This is your body, taken by me."

If you have an adoration chapel at your church or a chapel at your school, spend time there. It will help to purify your eyes and your memory. Be generous with your time. Consider that the average American spends a decade of his life watching TV! I'm inviting you not only to spend a few minutes in front of the tabernacle but to spend years of your life in adoration!

5. Use personal prayer.

In the words of one young man, "The way one treats a woman corresponds to the way one lives with God."[26] We will live as we pray, so if our prayer lives are weak, we will lack the strength to be pure. We may complain that purity is difficult, but how often do we ask God for the gift of purity? Especially when we feel tempted, we must have recourse to prayer. In

43

the words of Pope John Paul II, "Love . . . is victorious because it prays."[27]

Please pray for everyone who reads this booklet. Perhaps you can use a petition like that of Blessed Pier Giorgio Frassati, who asked a friend, "I beg you to pray for me a little, that God may give me an iron will that does not bend and does not fail in his projects."[28] By praying for each other in this way, we can form an army of men interceding for each other to grow in the love of God. To the degree that we love God and women, we will be pure.

6. Ask the saints for help.

I do not know of any man who lives a pure life without the help of others. We should take advantage of some of our greatest helpers: those who are in heaven. For starters, take up a greater devotion to your guardian angel. When you feel weak, ask your guardian angel for strength. He's not the overweight winged toddler you see on a Christian greeting card. He's a supernatural creature with immeasurable power to assist you. Unfortunately, we are all oblivious to our angels most of the time.

Take up a devotion to St. Joseph. Considering that the Church honors him as "Guardian of the Virgin" and "Terror of Demons," he's the ideal saint for young men.

Most important is a devotion to the Blessed Virgin Mary. It is essential as a Christian to have a personal relationship with Christ, but the Lord also wants us to get to know his Mother. There is a desire in every guy to have our masculinity affirmed by a woman. The more we feel drawn to a woman, the more we seek her approval. We want to please her, and we want to be seen as a man by her. There is one woman whose beauty surpasses all others, a woman who is the very essence of femininity. God himself chose her to be his Mother, and gave her to be the wife of the greatest male saint, Joseph. She is our Lady, the Virgin Mary.

Take up our Lady's weapon, the rosary. Always keep one in your pocket, and pray it daily. Ask her to teach you how to look at women. Ask her how she would have you treat her daughters. In the words of Pope John Paul II:

> My desire is for the young people of the entire world to come closer to Mary. . . . May young people have increasing confidence in her, and may they entrust the life just opening before them to her.[29]

Develop a true devotion to our Lady. You will make more progress under her protection than you would in years without her. Every single day, beg our Lady to grant you the grace of purity, and you will see why the saints have boundless confidence in her intercession.

Especially during moments of temptation, turn your eyes toward her. Entrust yourself to her, and you will see that nothing inspires masculinity as much as being in the presence of true femininity.

7. Fast.

St. Josemaria Escriva said that "gluttony is the fore-runner of impurity."[30] If we can learn to control our appetites when it comes to food, we will be better able to control our sexual desires. Instead of the desires of the body dominating the soul, the soul will control the body. As Pope John Paul II said, "The satisfaction of the passions is one thing, and the joy that man finds in mastering himself more fully is another thing."[31]

Consider the pain people put themselves through to have perfect bodies, including workouts, diets, and plastic surgery. Yet we resist the idea of suffering to perfect our souls.

But fasting is not only a tool to help gain self-mastery; it is a powerful spiritual weapon. During an exorcism, Jesus said, "This kind cannot be driven out by anything but prayer and fasting" (Mark 9:29). Praying for purity without fasting for it is like boxing with one arm tied behind your back. This verse also tells us that the graces that come from fasting can be offered up for others.

Our sexual urge is a source of energy; it cannot be repressed, but it must be channeled somewhere. An effective way to deal with temptation is to replace it with a task. For example, offer up a fast for women. A great resource to help you do this is www.e5men.org, where you can join thousands of other men making the same sacrifice.

If you are unsure about how to fast, talk to a holy priest. His wisdom will guide your generous efforts.

8. Do something.

"Flee idleness," St. Robert Bellarmine warned, "for no one is more exposed to such temptations than he who has nothing to do."[32] It is important that we keep busy and not get bored and feel sorry for ourselves. Practice a sport, go out with friends, serve the Church. Do something. As St. Francis of Assisi said, "Always be doing something worthwhile, then the devil will always find you busy."[33]

9. Control your eyes and words.

The eyes are the windows to the soul, and they are constantly challenged. The book of Sirach tells us:

> Turn away your eyes from a shapely woman, and do not look intently at beauty belonging to another; many have been misled by a woman's beauty, and by it passion is kindled like a fire. (Sir. 9:8)

Looking away is not our final goal. The reason for looking away is not that the woman's body is bad but that we're weak. It gives us time to reconsider what is valuable in a woman. Christ did not die for us so that we could spend the rest of our lives avoiding the sight of beautiful women. He came to transform our hearts so that we would be able to see her as God sees her. If his redemption of our hearts were not real, the Christian life would be unbearable. But with a real change of heart, we will, for example, feel pity for prostitutes instead of lust. Our sexual desires will not disappear. They will be elevated.

With this inner transformation, we will not only look at women differently, we will change the way we speak of them. Pure words flow from a pure heart and disclose the thoughts of a pure mind.

Having pure speech does not mean always talking about chastity. More often than not, it means holding back a crude joke or a comment about a woman passing by. Perhaps St. John Vianney said it best when he described a man of impure speech as a "person whose lips are but an opening and a supply pipe that hell uses to vomit its impurities upon the earth."[34]

Being a gentleman is not an act you play when you're in the presence of a woman. No matter how charming and polite you are around girls, if you sound like Howard Stern when you're with the guys, then you are no gentleman. In the words of the book of Sirach, "A man who has the habit of abusive language will never mature in character as long as he lives" (Sir. 23:15, NAB). If you don't control your words, you'll never control your body.

10. Exercise patient perseverance.

Imagine being the baseball player who holds the record for having struck out the most times or the basketball player who missed 9,000 shots in his career, twenty-six of them potential game-winners. It sounds like these guys are losers, but these are the stats of Babe Ruth and Michael Jordan. They knew that the more you practice a particular sport, the easier the skills to succeed become. The same is true of purity. With practice and patience, virtue becomes easier to live.

This is why St. Paul assured us that "in all these things we conquer overwhelmingly through him who loved us" (Rom. 8:37, NAB). There is no need to give in to discouragement or despair if you fall. Be patient with yourself. Pope John Paul II said that "chastity is a difficult, long term matter; one must wait patiently for it to bear fruit, for the happiness of loving kindness that it must bring. But at the same time, chastity is the sure way to happiness."[35] If you think that's a bold promise, test his words for yourself.

"Is purity really possible?"

Every man has the ability to be pure. Most lack only the motivation. Where is that going to come from?

I've heard it said that a knight cannot be brave unless he has love. His love gives him his courage.

Whether it's love of his queen, his family, his country, or freedom, this driving force overpowers his fear of defeat and death. The knight can stare death in the face not because he cares little about life but because he cherishes it. This passionate love keeps him from fleeing the battlefield.

In the same way, a man cannot be pure unless he has love. His love for God and women gives him his courage. Because of this love, he chooses a sacrificial path that may bring mockery and rejection. He turns down countless opportunities for selfish pleasure not because he lacks love for women but because his love for them is so strong. He is not pure because he lacks passion. It is his passion that fuels his purity.

It is possible for you to be pure if you want it. A man can be abstinent by accident (for example, lack of opportunity), but you cannot be pure without freely choosing the lifestyle and fighting to preserve it. This is difficult, but what noble and good thing is not? And what's the alternative to chastity? A life of sloth, mediocrity, and living for one's self? That is not living; it's merely existing.

Some may say, "Why not just go with the flow and give in to what feels natural?" Try this attitude in sports, and you'll never make the team. Try it in academics, and you'll never attend college. Try it in marriage, and divorce will be inevitable. Try it as a father, and your children will resent you. We have been made to live for something greater than ourselves.

If you wish to be pure, begin by admitting your need for grace. Purity is a gift from Jesus Christ, and he will give it to you if you ask for it with faith, humility, and perseverance. You have what it takes, because you are a son of God.

Prayer for Purity by St. Thomas Aquinas

Dearest Jesus! I know well that every perfect gift, and above all others that of chastity, depends upon the most powerful assistance of thy Providence, and that without thee a creature can do nothing. Therefore, I pray thee to defend, with thy grace, chastity and purity in my soul as well as in my body. And if I have ever received through my senses any impression that could stain my chastity and purity, do thou, who art the supreme Lord of all my powers, take it from me, that I may with an immaculate heart advance in thy love and service, offering myself chaste all the days of my life on the most pure altar of thy divinity. Amen.

St. Joseph, Guardian of the Virgin, pray for us.
St. Joseph, Terror of Demons, pray for us.
Immaculate Heart of Mary, pray for us.

1   John Eldredge, *Wild at Heart* (Nashville: Thomas Nelson Publishers, 2001), 62.
2   John Paul II, "We Wish to See Jesus," Feb. 22, 2004.
3   Robert E. Rector, et al. *The Harmful Effects of Early Sexual Activity and Multiple Sexual Partners Among Women: A Book of Charts*, Heritage Foundation, June 26, 2003 (available at www.heritage.org).
4   St. John Chrysostom, *Homilies on Ephesians*, 20,8.
5   St. Augustine, *Confessions*, VIII.
6   D. Zillman and J. Bryant, "Pornography's Impact on Sexual Satisfaction," *Journal of Applied Social Psychology* 18 (1988), 438–453.
7   John Paul II, *The Theology of the Body* (Boston: Pauline Books and Media, 1997), 346.
8   St. Josemaria Escriva, *The Way* (New York: Scepter, 2001), 40.
9   John Paul II, *Mulieris Dignitatem*, 14.
10 St. Alphonsus Liguori, *The Dignities and Duties of the Priest*.
11 Karol Wojtyła, *The Way to Christ* (San Francisco: Harper, 1982), 55–56.
12 P. Cameron and K. Cameron, "Homosexual Parents," *Adolescence* 31, Winter 1996, 757–76.
13 National Institutes of Health, "Scientific Evidence on Condom Effectiveness for Sexually Transmitted Disease (STD) Prevention" (June, 2000), 26. (www.niaid.nih.gov/dmid/stds/condomreport.pdf).
14 C. Sonnex, S. Strauss, and J. J. Gary, "Detection of Human Papillomavirus DNA on the Fingers of Patients with Genital Warts," *Sexually Transmitted Infections*, vol. 7:5 (1999): 317–319.
15 Centers for Disease Control and Prevention, "Prevention of Genital Human Papillomavirus Infection," Report to Congress, Jan. 2004, 3.

16 Centers for Disease Control and Prevention, *Prevention of Genital HPV Infection and Sequelae: Report of an External Consultants' Meeting*, December 1999 (available at www.cdc.gov).

17 *Catechism of the Catholic Church* 2339.

18 Thomas of Celano, *The First Life of St. Francis of Assisi*, chapter LXXXIII.

19 Eldredge, *Wild at Heart*, 184.

20 Karol Wojtyła, *Love and Responsibility* (San Francisco: Ignatius Press, 1993), 135.

21 St. Josemaria Escriva, *The Way*, 40.

22 John Paul II, *Redemptor Hominis*, 10.

23 Michael Collopy, *Works of Love Are Works of Peace* (San Francisco: Ignatius, 1996), 53.

24 John Paul II, "We Wish to See Jesus."

25 St. John Chrysostom, homily 46 on the Gospel of John.

26 Philippe Lefebvre, "*Les livres de Samuel et les récits de résurrection*," Paris, Cerf.

27 John Paul II, *The Theology of the Body*, 376.

28 Pasquale Di Girolamo, S.J., *Blessed Pier Giorgio Frassati* (New Hope, Ky.: St. Martin de Porres Lay Dominican Community, 1990), 46.

29 John Paul II, *The Meaning of Vocation* (Princeton, N.J.: Scepter Publishers, 1997), 33.

30 St. Josemaria Escriva, *The Way*, 41.

31 John Paul II, *The Theology of the Body*, 213–214.

32 St. Robert Bellarmine, *The Art of Dying Well*, as quoted in R. E. Guiley, *The Quotable Saint*, 135.

33 St. Francis of Assisi, as quoted in Paul Thigpen, *A Dictionary of Quotes from the Saints* (Ann Arbor, Mich.: Charis Books, 2001), 123.

34 St. John Vianney, as quoted in Guiley, *The Quotable Saint*, 226.

35 Wojtyła, *Love and Responsibility*, 172.

"THE HOUR YOU WERE THERE CHANGED MY LIFE FOREVER!"

Spend an hour with Jason and Crystalina Evert

After a year of speaking as an engaged couple, Jason and Crystalina married in June 2003, and continue to share their inspirational testimonies with hundreds of thousands of teens and parents internationally. In their highly popular chastity seminar, "Romance without Regret," the duo provides compelling and uplifting reasons for embracing the virtue of chastity.

Some think that chastity simply means, "not having sex." But that's mere abstinence: what you can't do and can't have. Chastity is more than that; it is about what you can do and have, right now: a chaste lifestyle that brings freedom, respect, peace, and romance-without regret.

What can save the marriages of tomorrow? In an age in which the media tell young people that they cannot–and need not– control themselves sexually, Jason and Crystalina's message to students from junior high school on up is challenging, entertaining, encouraging, and healing. Get the healthy male and female perspectives on living chastely as you listen to their life-changing message.

For more information on hiring Jason and Crystalina
share their message, contact our Seminars Coordinator
at 619-387-7200 or visit www.chastity.com

Chastity.com
The New Sexual Revolution Is Here.

Hook-ups, friends with benefits, safe sex, and now safer sex? Our generation found out the hard way that none of it gives us the love we long for.

Romance without regret does exist. But if you want the real thing, be prepared to sacrifice. Only then will you see that the peace and joy that come from chastity is worth more than all the pleasures of the world.

Within the pages of www.chastity.com, you are going to find blunt, honest, and uplifting reasons for why you're worth waiting for. No fear tactics. No guilt trips. Just the demands of authentic human love.